SEA LION CAVES

and other

poems

ams press
new york

SEA LION CAVES

and other poems

Nelson Bentley

NEW POETRY SERIES

Alan Swallow, Denver

Library of Congress Cataloging in Publication Data

Bentley, Nelson.
    Sea lion caves.

    Reprint of the 1966 ed. published by A. Swallow, Denver,
in series: New poetry series.
    I. Title.
[PS3552.E55S4   1975]   811'.5'4   70-179835
ISBN 0-404-56035-0
        0-404-56000-8 (SET)

The New Poetry Series

Reprinted by arrangement with
The Swallow Press Inc.
Copyright © 1966 by Nelson Bentley
First AMS edition published in 1975
AMS Press Inc. 56 E. 13th St.
New York, N.Y. 10003

Manufactured in the USA

145006

For BETH, SHAWN, and JULIAN

Many of these poems have appeared in *New World Writing, Poetry London-New York, Poetry* (Chicago), *Beloit Poetry Journal, Modern Age, Talisman, Colorado Quarterly, Prairie Schooner, Western Humanities Review, Experiment, University of Kansas City Review, Michigan Quarterly Review, Colorado Review, Whetstone, Fiddlehead, Views, American Weave, Coastlines,* and the anthology *Ten Poets: Seattle, 1962.*

CONTENTS

ATGET'S LENS

Final turning of a place to poem,
A lone vision to a textured home,
      And look to book;
Who'd think to find you in a photograph,
Perfectly quiet in the arrested chaff:
      A love that took?

A lettered wagon tired in early light,
A snarling knocker that will never bite,
      Transformed tokens,
Answer for an old brown grateful Paris
That entered intact the rare, knowing iris
      Of Atget's lens.

A peddler sedate on steep-slanted bricks,
Trees waving in twenty great gold clocks,
      Dummies' proud stance:
All waited for James' pen or Atget's mounts.
It's the selection on which love counts,
      The surest glance.

City and heart sing this humble realm,
An ardor that clears away the film.
      Order is all;
Its constant surprise is where it will appear,
Implying the search that makes an atmosphere
      Or a total.

SESTINA

Scarcely imaginable the enormous circle
Swings through wildernesses none can range,
I thought at seven standing in the leafsmoke,
Except with one whose hair is deep as eyes,
With whom can be found the sun-drenched tower
Where love waits in an illuminated book.

Finding that so few knew of the book
My unmentioned trek started toward the circle
And smally passed by many a cold dim tower.
My heart shook beside their lightless range
But sensed discovery of a crown of eyes
And knew obscurity not the aim of smoke.

Each fall created arrows of sharp smoke
Wafting toward the leaves of the towered book
To wrap it in a redolence of eyes.
Could it be the eyes were the circle,
The wilderness easy to arrange?
What was the distance to the crucial tower?

By brilliant solitudes I soon saw tower
A subtle flower above the sumached smoke:
Castle of the tall Mozartian range
Where sorrow knelt rejoicing in the book.
In gay andante my heart spun the circle
To make each act as full as early eyes.

And to my love came instantly those eyes
In which the pupils know the light-told tower.
Lonely faith had synonymed the circle.
Become the fire of the far October smoke.
The leaves hailed like prisms to the book.
It was a way of looking took the range.

Rose-deep, two loves in light now daily range
Their acts by rule of the crown of eyes
Brimmed by an illuminated book.
Two solitudes lift the light-tall tower
In landscapes more than legend, where leafsmoke
Rings with sarabands a once-wild circle.

The years are eyes that fill with the gay circle.
Through fall's blue smoke, center of all range,
Tower the lines of the discovered book.

THE RAVEN IN NEW ORLEANS

(For Lafcadio Hearn)

With Poe in one slim hand,
Ragged black hair, weird eye, you stand
While through dim Cincinnati wings the crow
Of your unique sorrow
To perch as clown deep in your ardent mind.

Loti and Baudelaire
Saved you with scents of Malabar;
Since you were true, intense, odd and bereft,
Poverty and a gift
Opened love's books and your books found you there.

Tar, coco-oil and musk,
A tent of blue hair, a life's task,
Sailed your close gaze to the *Thompson Dean's*
Docking at New Orleans:
The quadroon bit a mango just at dusk;

Then grew the endless look
That builds a window with a book.
Ebony set the raven's diadem
And lit each day's *Item*:
The queer quills flew on fragrant isles of folk.

From musked and mangoed rain
Serenely rose the great blue crane,
Whose ragged agent rode each mail's margin
With notes for old Watkin:
The ageless wader pointed toward Japan.

12

The raven saw him flown
And carved one voyage on the crown,
Then gave it to the wise hands brown and broad
Of his Muse of the Odd
And flew to Fuji's faultless dream-pure cone.

Lafcadio, the look
That bumped your nose on every book
In Hawkins' shop, the raven's eye and crown
Will always rule the crane:
The Muse of the Odd knew it at Martinique.

THE WOOD

Let all encounters praise
The wooded ways
Whose trees were candles from a foreknown tower;
Who would adore
Have clearly known the heights of dark.

Where by an inland sea
Humility
Weltered the high waves of a proud sad will,
Intensely still
It carved regret into the bark.

As circling gull's flight faith
Lit like a breath
The bleak reaches of a stoic shore:
The will therefore
Attained its ceremonial.

Walked new the wood of books
And holy works:
Childhood's visions, found, came down in showers,
As plum flowers
From a maturity will fall.

The wood with wonder rinsed
A love advanced,
A realm of light topped by the clear tower.
All time before
Illumined comes from where it will.

RICERCAR

The sun-enamelled hills of awe,
   Cresting the blue
Lake, found their brilliance in a flaw
Made sound. The woods of Washtenaw
Went red as legend as the wasteful eye saw true.

  Each siloed and cow-spangled lodge,
   Wheat on a cloud,
Trees shriven in October smudge,
The windows of a well-worn Dodge
Washed into emblems. Where the willow's attitude

  Folded in focal calm had spun
   With Mozart's flute
A skein of adoration,
The heart curved with the still Huron
Through fugues alight with faith tranquil and convolute.

  The Delhi falls burned into paint,
   Each elm a vase.
So fully did the eye acquaint
To find the love that makes a point,
And reconcile the flaw that antedates a face.

VILLANELLE

Oaks and garrets lit the folding dusk.
The candle melted in the closing day.
Eyes weltered in nostalgia's musk.

Across the chimneys Schubert's arabesque
Wove a sad love that nothing else could say.
Oaks and garrets lit the folding dusk.

Pure years came together in a brusque
Illumined parting that is time's full way.
Eyes weltered in nostalgia's musk,

Seeing for last and first the plain grotesque
Midwestern architecture in decay:
Oaks and garrets lit the folding dusk.

When the old Dodge parked forever, dented husk
Of poverty's long defining and delay,
Eyes weltered in nostalgia's musk;

A train would come at morning for the task.
Love's touch must be most casual in goodbye:
Oaks and garrets lit the folding dusk,
Eyes weltered in nostalgia's musk.

BALLADE

Rainier and daisies shared a core;
Gulls wove caesuras slow as snow.
Aloof poises of Zanzibar
Counterpointed sad Thoreau.
Decades screened in pale willow
The pastel slopes of prayer climb
As knees and eyes begin to know
The pattern is the end of time.

Candle light on skins of tar,
Ocean's steady wash of woe,
Tennyson sobbing by the bar,
Loss-telling Joyce, shy Cyrano,
The mingled wings of gull and crow
Rejoice in brilliant antonym
When reconciliations grow:
The pattern is the end of time.

Coherence, love's far Malabar,
Tumbles each Malvolio;
The dull night sees despair's dim star
Flare with interested Marlowe.
Hearn found he needed Tokyo;
Opposites are ardor's rim.
I kneel colored by all I owe:
The pattern is the end of time.

Envoy

Decades screened in pale willow
The pastel slopes of prayer climb
As knees and eyes begin to know
The pattern is the end of time.

AT THE MOUTH OF GRAY'S HARBOR

The eye's heart is to hope the moments mend.
At high tide I and Shakespeare sensed the shore.
In sequent toil all forwards do contend.

Dark interweaving wishes jostling wend
Toward their last melancholy breaking roar:
The eye's heart is to hope the moments mend.

Our wrestle with the hours is to defend
Sweet repetition's unimagined more
In sequent toil. All forwards do contend

Cross purposes the knees must comprehend.
Sequence is the what art must adore.
The eye's heart is to hope. The moments mend

When pupils have looked clearly at the end.
The contrapuntal now, the splendid spoor,
In sequent toil all forwards do contend.

Time tosses us our casual stipend:
The curious light inside a metaphor.
The eye's heart is to hope the moments mend.
In sequent toil all forwards do contend.

PHASES OF RAINIER

Ghost
Afloat
In the most lost
Time: omitted remote
Acts of love: unaccounted cost:
Old thinking cap: pearl-sailed, swan-swaddled boat:
Egret of plunge and plume: scarred, flaw-flushed, embossed

Cone
That points
All the undone:
Antithesis of haunts:
Slopes reuniting the alone:
Manito the beaded moccasin tints:
Tangible trace: inestimable potlatch: bone,

Tooth
And shell
Sewn to our youth
To ornament the will:
White counterpoise to a brief breath:
Ancient refrain, wings of the syllable:
Cold, clear, intense ascent, asking neither or both.

ODE TO MEMORY

The owl in welkins of old time
Folds his deep tree
With the weird sisters' cloak and spell.
The country school floats on a damasked sea;
The shelves of Hawthorne are a loom.
Old hope haunts sleepy horns
That bellow slow by moon and buoy
A sad love reconciled to doom.
The Cascades' time-aloof blue bourns
Are the school bell
That summoned me at six, books' new envoy.
Cool on the coal barn's roof
That rode dismay like a red ark
I heard the omened hoof
Of eohippus in my head.
Clear dread
Rich as Arabia adorns
The sequent years.
Memory: complex repair:
Insatiable linkage of Good Hope and Horn:
Illustrious repeat the ears adore:
Knot of keen cares:
Congress of illusions: diminished bark
Whose fading sail summons the flown:
Ruffling hoot: hone:
Quick ruins where ghosts go to work.
Faith flares when we can recapitulate
Early or late
An owl-deep, unchanged, ordained wariness.

I acquiesce,
Sole key
To appearance and reality.
The past is all the light below the lash.
The days are ash
In a cyclone unless
Calm memory
Fills each grain with a love that will atone,
And actions fall
Into the real world Shakespeare had long known
Writing *Ripeness is all*.

SARABAND

India spreads its saris in her wrists;
     Her footsole prints
    The silver convoluted twists
    Of jewel boxes. Sandalwood
And ebony surround her hair's black tents.
    Persia purls her blood.

Eyes serenely carved in Chinese jades
     As calm as swans
    Swim where the envied heron wades
    In Yangtzes of acceptance: still
Savage grace like toothed and beaded skins
    Threads a Byzantine skill

 From long ago by the shores of the Black Sea.
     Hebraic one
    Whose nose adores antiquity,
    Dark face where all museums clink,
She rested in the mind of Solomon
    When song began to think.

MEDITATION

             The   vow - white   crests
             Of   jagged   Cascades,
             Gate - hinge   behests
             Of   gulls,   slow   braids
             Of   drifting   wings,
             Hem   suffering's
Rich   trim   around   the   illumined   panels   of   old   love:
The   days   emerge   in   a   density   of   adoration.
When   time's   wing   has   been   seen   silken   as   Cowper's   dove,
Lineaments   ignite   in   a   complex   contrition.
             Far   boat - horns'   peal,
             Dawn   winds'   white   touch,
             Translate   a   weal
             The   eye   can   reach.
             In   the   knee's   move
             Abides   Whale   Cove:
             In   a   false   look
             Will   Chinook   Pass
             Collapse   in   ash.
             A   wiry   brook
             Praises   the   edge
             Of   true   image.

THE CROWS

With slow flaps out of a childhood night
    Crooked as road-repairing tar
        Two anthracite
    Crows light, a single avatar
Daily on a madrona branch. My throat

Recalls those rasping caws that thickly float
    A long-used oil over the leaves,
        The hoarse, harsh note
    Roughening who untimely grieves.
Calm, glossy and inseparable they sit

Gay, rocky shadows in the ruffling green.
    Besides Macbeth's thick rooky thought
        And Poe's obscene
    Rooms where writhed his absolute,
Through Smart, Blake, Coleridge, Hearn these two
                    have flown.

Their caws are an alarm. Black wings unfold
    Centers of dogwood and of rose.
        Sad days annulled
    Garland the ragged flight. The crows
And songbirds sit small, clear and reconciled.

THE EYE

The eye must leave and shape
A home of wind: cast its peculiar mote
Anchored as the Olympics: make its ship
        A heron's throat.
    Must slowly take the grain of shell,
    Bark, shore, devoutly marginal.

A SUMMER RAIN

Moss-mottled maples veiled
In rain light as a floating swallow
In wet wefts fold
Fingers of willow.
Paused robins hear the subtle squirm
Of worm.

A wet crow slowly bends
Rough wings up to a high dead branch
Above the wind's
Bright avalanche.
An air of surf, whale spouts and shells
Uncells

The breath of grass and rose.
The slender sail-horns like a flute
Or flower close
In a bright mute.
Deep in each falling drop is wound
The sound.

THE OLYMPICS

Faith lit those clefts and cones. The cinctured sharp
                    Fullness of time
Dances the distant blue. The heart's old warp
                    Lives in the trim
        Of the longest wish. David and all
                Subsequent pages sail
In that snowy light where the world's colors fold
                And the twice told

Tales saturate the ear with hope. High gulls
                Float past The Brothers,
Changeless above the old oak's reddening falls,
                Whiter than feathers,
        Fairer than Olympus. Eyes
                Buoyed on all that dies
Enclose, to open on a touch that grows
                Felicitous.

TIGERS AND LAMBS

Crisp sift of yellow past accepting limbs,
Cool wisdom's season blows the eyelid wide
Almost as childhood: Blake's tigers and lambs
      Dance on a latitude.

Wheeled in the forest of his earliest fall,
Shawn's touch is soft and trustful as a rose:
His eye contains our love as a petal
      Knows what it cannot lose.

May the robin singing in the maple's maze
Of moss and yellow light, the drifted leaf,
Fill his look ever with his shy amaze,
      His sharp starts save the deaf.

Squirrels dislodge the hesitant motif:
Blossoms have rustled into myth. The mind
Shaped by the product of its true belief
      Must lift praise to the end,

Inseparable from the old command.
Happier by every acrid stack,
It wreathes song cycles on a bluer wind.
      In nights tinged by the bleak

White birches wither. The Olympic peaks
Hold half way out of time the whitest snows,
Which, in the hour the tiger-clear sun talks,
      Will melt into a rose.

PINE

Two pine trees made a ritual of rain.
Fragrant needles repairing a rent sky
Cradled in their sinews hyaline
All ancient tears' habitual embassy.

                To pine, to pine,
Is properly to yearn to illumine.

Well up in the Cascade Range a cataract
In a world of pine makes a quadruple plunge
Whose white tumult is a changeless pact.
Green awes of childhood awake awash,

                Well up, well up,
And, poised by pine, unite all start and stop.

THE BONE

A gnawed, blood-tinted bone
On a dandelioned lawn
Lay like a storm-flung shell
Or a lost syllable,
And I saw in a light antique
My dog of boyhood, Mike,
Half airedale, half collie,
With wag-tailed melancholy
Savor it under a peach
Twenty years out of reach.
I saw our ardent, meek
Research along Elm Creek
In sunny synagogues
Of cat-tails, crabs and frogs
Where his soft scholarly barks
Caused wild amphibian arcs,
His lifted ears and paw
Controlled by what I knew:
And I saw I had understood
In that croaking, froggy odd
Clear as in rose or dove
Imponderable love.

SIGHTSEEING

Aloft on the salmon's home
At the worn rail we watched
The piers fade into frame
In the hour of the disattached.
Our eyes looked over the cold
Waves from a sunlit fold:
Father's, mother's and son's
And three motionless nuns'.

Skyscrapers shrank to pins,
The bay a fragile cup.
All of man's environs
From the Flood and the Sphinx up
Curled in the mountain chains.
As our eyes met the nuns'
We saw from sea to shore
The circle of ardor.

THE SEAMEW

A seamew's moil aweave in mossy oaks
Moved on my eye a keen and linen sail,
As a plum branch with recollection chokes
               So springs not fail.

A wind of snow lines waved the daffodils.
Wing-white, plum-petal dense, a poem's ground,
Birches achieved their early syllables,
               Worship ingrained.

THE LEAF

Yellow leaf immure
This adoration pure,
Transmute into a page
From exaltation sage;
For the end of nature
Is to show love's texture.
Skin tensile as a pear
Where the world's orchards are
Pressed in a lone contour,
Apothegm aflare
Floated on frosted air,
Legible as a birch
And intense as a torch,
You love the ardent eye
As time does poetry.

THE *ILLAHEE*

Ships almost lost on stretches of blue
        By blue islands
            Breathe a frail lavender smoke;
        On the ferry *Illahee*, a flake,
            We watch at a white rail the small hands
Of our son paused in his butterfly awe.

The Cascades keep rising over Seattle.
            Snowed crevices
            Delta into the clouds.
        In white unwavering attitudes
        Like herons on an ancient vase
The Brothers gaze across the swift and brittle.

Shawn in blue denim looks at the blue city
            In a wash of gulls
            And wishes toward a word.
        Below circles of blue accord
        Skyscrapers fragile as eggshells
Respond to the surpliced ferry's litany.

And the white summits chorus into praise.
            The *Illahee*
            Is Botticelli's shell
        Where Venus rides the slow sea swell.
        Love's eyes quicken eternity,
That snowy resonance of all our days.

THE SEAL

A raucous surf perplexed our ears.
A wind of pearl wailed on tufted dunes:
A tempest misted with Asia's tears,
                    The wash of love.
        Wave-worn, the wood of other Junes
Waited the tidal nudge. The placid gull
Soared on the buffeting inevitable.
                    As our eyes wove
        Shell, gull and wave, we saw the seal
Flopping in breakers, swept back up the sands,
Wrenching his flippers toward the water's weal.
                    We ran to lift
        Him, new-born, in our warm strange hands,
His bitten navel cord like a stuck-out tongue,
His white and black hair ready for the long
                    And chill spindrift.
        Black eyes abrim with gentleness
Gave us their whiskery, spelled, certain gaze
Wishing oceanward deeper than any guess.
                    A child's or saint's
        Eyes, and the center of a rose
Shared in that tangibility of trust;
Freshly as Hopkins we saw the Holy Ghost
                    Brood in the distance.

ON HAVING PUT OUR SMALL SON TO BED

The driftwood embers spit their dwindled sparks.
From ocean salt
Illumination waves on Vaughan's works;
Moby Dick, smiling, lurks
On the davenport
Among the mild flotilla of the tub.
Uncle Monkey,
Sage as Beatrix Potter, sees the nub
And sprawls upon a bib
Beatifically;
Zebra grazes on the Navaho rug
In gentle stance
Below the striped halo of a good-night hug.
Quick as a pollywog
In their long dance
"The weeping Pleiads wester;" the world is seen
"In a grain of sand,
And Heaven in a wild flower." Shawn sleeps between
Red Bear and O'Shaughnessy: one
Faith-gentle hand
Enfolds the small bear known as Christopher Smart,
As a rose holds scent.
He curls in our wished purity of heart,
The source and end of art
Made evident.

THE CONE

This pine cone fans its perpetual fable
As Haystack Rock
Shapes the ocean's syllable.
Definitive as a porcupine,
Augury of the adamantine,
It rests in the filmy seeds strewn on my desk:

Pale fish foiling in a childhood brook.
The touch adores
As purely as the look.
I remembered when our son,
Aged three, tendered me this cone
While seagulls' shadows climbed the sycamores.

PHOTOGRAPH

I am seven in this photograph.
My rumpled white
Collar frames a vigorously shy love
Unuttering as lamb, birch or swan.
I've just come from an ash's windy height
Or a vision.

That season the surge of boughs,
Leaves glossed with frost,
Winnowed me in the world's wood of books.
The old school's oily floors
Smelled of Aladdin; in shadowy Hawthorne lost
Were the whorls of my ears.

How purely we are told
Of love fulfilled.
It was a month ago child looked at child,
Communicants in sweet delay;
Holding the picture like a bird's egg, my son called,
"Mama, who is this little boy?"

SAND-DOLLARS

Since poets must live on the edge of the Infinite
We come more often to this vacant coast,
Fold in our ears the gulls' atonal flute
And find white sand-dollars, the never lost,
Each stitched with a star like the imprint of the Ghost.

We join a conspiracy of seals and clams.
Isaiah's rapture knew such cool surmise.
Our small son balances in driftwood realms;
Our cabin in the wind that doesn't cease
Illuminates the ultimate boundaries.

These starred dollars, a standard currency,
Are found where the wave-planed sand mirrors wings
In an odd clarity of light. Our child and we
In a sweet humbling of imaginings
Find clam shells to fit angels in old paintings.

WASHINGTON COAST

I stand on shards of clam while Shawn
Filling his circus pail with sand
Kneels in the shelter of a dune:
Gentle as a rose his hand
Scoops and lifts the fluted shell.
A monotone lives in the sedge,
A mile from any daffodil.
Beth, far down the ocean edge,
Hunts agates, imaged in the glaze:
Charms from underneath the tide.
Love impels me to compose.
Gulls knit the waves' infinitude.
Though I have shot no living thing
A hunting cap keeps warm my ears,
An ocean in the spiralling:
I aim a pencil down the years.

A FEW MILES BELOW SNOQUALMIE PASS

Eyes washed in the cascading element,
Face weathering with the corrugated firs,
I lead my son through moss and cedar scent
In the tactile vision of his four years,
And climbing past the lichen-tufted pines
I watch the miracle of recompense.

His fingers on the moss-sponged, corky bark
And gummed by aromatic twigs and cones
Are sure as hummingbirds; in his pure look
The chipmunks feed at his devotions.
A childhood forest white with parchment birch
Was my imagination's sacred perch.

Near Humpback Creek's ever impulsive plunge
Into the Snoqualmie, we two stand.
All morning, paper boats have sailed down range.
He puts an origin upon my hand.
I think of Moses by the burning bush.
The waters tumble down, serenely fresh.

SEA LION CAVES

Bellows surge heavy as the waves
Through a cavern chopped in basalt. Slippery
And ponderous as the ocean, sea lions lie
In a primeval stench, serene and fresh
From sensual wallows in the surf,

Growling, tawny, in Dantean sprawl,
Deep inside the cape. Light washes through
The cave mouth to the first mossed, salty stones
And over these whiskered faces that endure,
Dripping and sinewy from the last plunge.

Outside, we wind back up the precipice
High over the sea lions drenched in spray
Sunning on lesser brinks. Out in the sea
They sport titanically, rolling the great crests,
Supple, whiskered bulls in every wave.

I kneel on a grassy pinnacle,
Help my child heap his hands with dandelions
And pale green foxtails. The fishy smell
Of sea lions hangs above the ancient gorge:
My eyes have become the containing blue.

CANNON BEACH

Who love these rocks have studied to endure.
The tall waves roar
And break their whitest on those basalt snags:
Foam mounts like wings
Out of a sound unchanged since Genesis.

The ocean heaves the weight of time ashore:
The rocks stand sheer.
White seafowl slowly skim immobile nests.
Fish blue with warts,
Eyes glazed by water, swim under the blue surface.

Where one black monolith makes immortal thrust
And waves smash most,
Light like a halo holds the primitive tip.
From cape to cape
That rigid word orders the surge of chaos.

BON ODORI, SEATTLE

Before the dances, brightly kimonoed girls
Wearing clogs or keds are eating hot dogs
And ice cream bars below the pink and yellow
Paper lanterns and blowing green of trees:
Women of all ages, down to two, begin
Dancing then with fragile, formal grace.

I watch, desirous as Lafcadio Hearn,
The shy, solemn, smiling, delicate faces,
The gay auroral patience of the fans,
A ritual of tragic radiance.
Flowers slow-float a river of black hair.
The centuries gather gently in their hands.

Each performs differently the same
Motion, shaped by the sense of awe,
A visible infinity of grace.
A few men and boys in ancient costume
Step with exact and wiry vigor:
Some children dance in their baby shoes,

Desiring grace as reticent as the rose,
Devoutly spontaneous in their parents'
Rigorous form. Some too small to dance
Are held, costumed, in their mothers' arms,
As changeless love delineates Japan
Among the young, rain-fresh Seattle pines.

ZERO TIDE

I walked from our cabin into the wet dawn
To see the white caps modulating in,
The slow wash of the word in the beginning:
Wind on the bowing sedge seemed from Japan.
A cloud of sandpipers wavered above the dune,
Where surf spoke the permanence of sun.
Back inside, I sat on my son's bed
Where he sweetly slept, guarded by saints and poets,
Oceanic sunrise on his eyelids;
I whispered "Shawn, get up! It's a clamming tide,"
And thought of chill sand fresh from lowering waters,
Foam-bubbled frets across the hard-packed ridges.
"Shawn, it's a zero tide!" From a still second,
He came out of the covers like a hummingbird.
"Don't wake up Julian." In the pale blue light
He dressed with whirring silence, all intent.
Along the empty coast the combers hummed:
Sleepy gulls mewled in the clearing mist.
My wife and baby slept folded in singing calm,
Involuted by love as rose or shell.

With raincoats, pail and shovel we walked the gloss
Of the Pacific margin, over mirrored
Gull, mist and sandpiper to a sandbar
Fresh from the ebb, and covered with clam holes.
The salt swells sometimes washed our boots
As we quickly dug, dropped to our knees and clasped
Elbow-deep in ooze the struggling shells,
Each white clam-foot with its gripping tip
Muscling for lost silence below the surf.
We pulled their burnished shields up into light,
Sharp edges slicing the sucked sand.
Primordial words of the tidal floor,
They lay in our palms fresh as the gaze of God.
"If nothing lay more developed," Walt Whitman said,
"The quahaug in its callous shell were enough."
Shawn danced with his pail of lacquered clams,
Reflected like a sea-bird on the slick;
His laugh of delight made the rosy dawn.
The breakers slowly blued and swelled their caps;
Isaiah's angel brought the glowing coal.

THE SPOUTING HORN

I stood by the stone sea-wall at Depoe Bay
And watched that slowly quickening rage of waves
At high tide, with my son and one-year daughter.
Each elemental seventh ramming in
Sent the sea's tumult through the spouting horn,
A natural fissure in the heaps of basalt:
A stream shot skyward like a waterfall,
A Helicon that rode the wet horizon.

Love's witnesses looked back at Genesis:
The winged horse stamped on the basalt cliff:
Soul and sense spouted in the light
As when the Whirlwind spoke to Job's desire
The sensual particulars of Awe.
"Let the floods clap their hands," the Psalmist wrote.
I praised by the sea-wall, having been given
Poems and children, the holiest shapes of love.

STORIES

The June sun sank through sparrow song to the hill
And sent light through my three-year daughter's hair:
We sat still as birds on our brick porch sill.

She told me stories of Ephelant and Bear,
Hippopomanus and Cock-a-doodle-doo:
Pensive as Aurora, she moved near.

The scene was familiar: in 1922
The sun hung low above the Elm Woods
And I was three, grandfather seventy-two.

We watched toward those leafy solitudes
Across a mile of creek and clovered meadow.
The old white porch filled with Ireland's moods

As we told stories in the maple shadow.
That same summer I stand in a knitted suit,
Hands full of dandelions, joyous in a photo.

The bees are climbing clover in slant light
Through which my joyous daughter, Julian,
Comes with her hands full of love's insight

Compacted at present in a dandelion.
In it the years are listening and still.
She frowns at it with sacred Imagination.

THE ROSE OF THE WORLD

As birds give all the kinds of light their names
And trees reach multitudinously into rain,
As seeds in fragrant blizzards sow the wind
And clear currents are known by the minnow's nose,
So does my mind continually praise.

As starfish cluster on the deepest piers,
Sea lions repose on a heaving surf
That carves their caves in the basalt cliff,
As mountains know the infinite by force,
So does my sense continually praise.

As Index and Pilchuck continually pierce
The wisdom of the light that folds the world,
As the seed multiplies the primal spell,
As the spouting horn lifts ocean into space,
So does my soul continually praise.

As imagination, soul and sense
Become as one in poetry and love,
My dear is the light in which I move,
The mystic center of the world's rose:
So do my poems continually praise.

THE LUMMI RESERVATION

I wade the sound knee-deep in a clear tide
Among the oyster shells and young starfish,
The chuckle and squawk of gulls, worn fishing boats,
The animal spirits of water, wood and sun,
Swimming blue shadows on sea-weeded shores,
And watch across the waves where Lummi Island
Lies quiescent as a basking whale
Or the intense repose of a totem pole.

A mile from here Hillaire carved his totems,
Compressing a bright legend in a log,
Small epics of courage and desire:
His sign a whale black as his ragged beard,
The potent tail curved into a circle.
His last, unfinished project fills my thought,
Each sacred, alert and solemn symbol:
The twenty four Animal Spirits in high council.

From the throat of each an Indian looked out,
Awed by the ultimate in all its forms,
Folded in nature's infinite metaphor,
A soul delighted in the law of sense:
So each of twenty four single wills were wrapped
In divine wisdom's necessary pelt.
He gave me Eagle to put above my books,
Vision in integrity white as Shuksan.

In primitive rapture the intellect takes shape.
Blake saw poetic genius as the Holy Ghost.
And Roethke's cry, Whitman's barbaric yawp,
Watkins with Taliesin on the Welsh coast,
Cummings in mountains of eternal now,
Are astonished as Job: "Now my eye sees Thee."
Those Animals came from the Whirlwind, Hillaire,
Fresh with the vision that sees everywhere.

ON TEACHING A NEW COURSE: "AMERICAN
LITERATURE SINCE 1930"

The manna floated steadily by our window
That winter evening in Michigan in 1930,
Where my sister Margaret and I played Authors.
We heard the kitchen door, Dad stamping snow.
"Don't have it." "Give me *The House of Seven Gables*."
We heard the words "X-ray," "tuberculosis,"
And, wondering, came upon their slow embrace.
"Oh, mama, will you die?" we cried, together,
And there by the smoking kerosene stove
The four of us clung like dogwood petals.

Six months before, while I fished on Deer Lake,
My father rowed, reciting Tennyson,
And his closest boyhood friend, Ed Corwin,
Described the joys of Constitutional Law,
Pulling perch, bass and sunfish from the waves:
We floated on intellectual delight.
And on the shore, among the parchment birch,
My mother waved, beside the old log lodge,
Between the deer horns and the bobcat skins,
Fragile and shy, between the arrowheads.

For fourteen years, then, her sacrificial love
Filled our white farmhouse like a radiance.
She read her Bible between the gentle Christ
And a blue-wash watercolor of the Rockies;
In one of her faded dresses, while picking berries,
She saw the burning bush in our raspberry patch
And wore her suffering lightly as a rose.
Between hospital trips, her worn piano
Sent Chopin and Mozart floating through the maples,
And the bookcases listened on every wall.

"Give me John Greenleaf Whittier's *Snowbound*."
And all since then's a literary era:
It grew in my memory, from the seed.
Then gather, poets, at that winter's table;
On Deer Lake, and in our raspberry patch:
Give me *Four Quartets* and *New Year Letter*,
One Times One, and *Words For The Wind*.
Imagination is Eternity, said Blake.
Without poetic vision there is no love.
Time is known only as a sacrament.